MICROWAVES

by Tracy Vonder Brink

PEBBLE
a capstone imprint

Pebble Emerge is published by Pebble, an imprint of Capstone.
1710 Roe Crest Drive
North Mankato, Minnesota 56003
www.capstonepub.com

Library of Congress Cataloging-in-Publication Data is available on the Library of Congress website.
ISBN: 978-1-9771-2271-1 (library binding)
ISBN: 978-1-9771-2617-7 (paperback)
ISBN: 978-1-9771-2298-8 (eBook PDF)

Summary: Microwaves are all around us, even if we don't see them. Learn all about microwaves and how we use them every day.

Image Credits
Capstone Studio: Karon Dubke, 20; iStockphoto: robypangy, 9, SpiffyJ, 17 (left); Shutterstock: anek.soowannaphoom, 16, Color4260, 14, Designua, 11, foto500, 19, glenda, 5, Grisha Bruev, 7, NatalyLad, 18, pedrosala, Cover, RaksyBH, 17 (right), sutham, 15, VaLiza, 13

Design Elements
Capstone; Shutterstock: file404, Miloje

Editorial Credits
Editor: Michelle Parkin; Designer: Ted Williams; Media Researcher: Jo Miller; Production Specialist: Laura Manthe

Printed and bound in China.
3322

TABLE OF CONTENTS

Words in **bold** are in the glossary.

WAVES

Hold one end of a jump rope. Ask a friend to hold the other side. Move it up and down. You made the rope move in waves!

Light moves in waves. A microwave oven heats food with special light waves. The waves are called microwaves. A microwave is a kind of light that you cannot see.

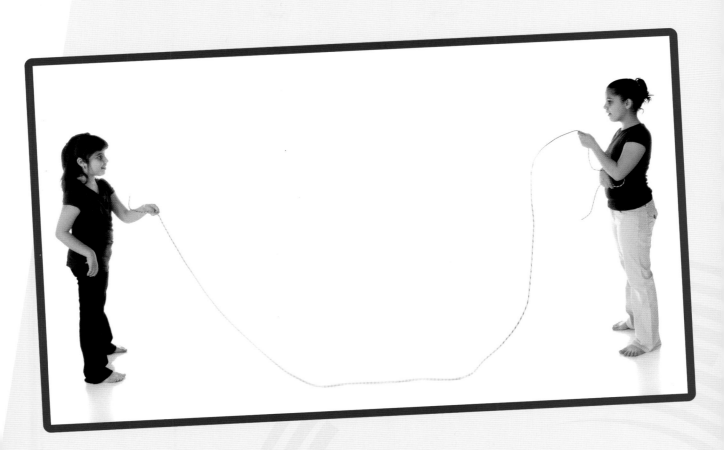

MOVING LIGHT

Look up at the sky at night. You see the light from stars. Light is a kind of **energy**. The sun and stars send out light energy.

Light travels in tiny particles called **photons**. The photons wiggle as they go. That makes the light move in waves.

WAVES THAT COOK

It's snack time. Dad puts a popcorn bag in the microwave oven. He pushes the button. Soon you have a yummy snack. But how?

A microwave oven is a metal box. Its walls keep the waves inside. The oven changes **electricity** into microwaves.

9

The waves in a microwave oven move up and down. They bounce off the walls. They do not bounce off the food inside. The waves move through the food.

Food has water inside. Even if you can't see it, a small amount of water is in the food. Microwaves make the water **vibrate** and heat up. The heat cooks the food.

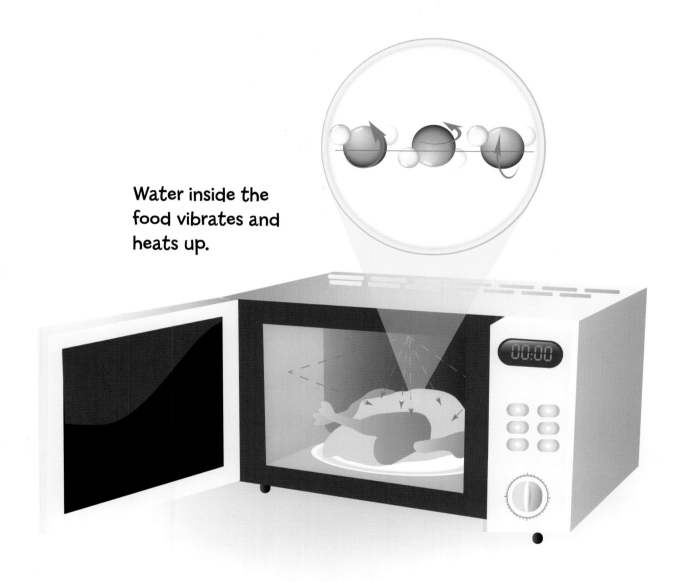

Water inside the food vibrates and heats up.

WAVES THAT CALL

What else can microwaves do? Have you talked on a cell phone? You were using microwaves! Microwaves carry messages between phones.

What happens when you call a friend? The phone changes your voice into a **signal**. Microwaves send it through the air. They travel fast.

The call goes from your phone to a special tower. The tower sends the signal to another tower. Your call travels until it reaches your friend's phone.

Your friend answers the phone. Your friend's phone sends a signal back to you.

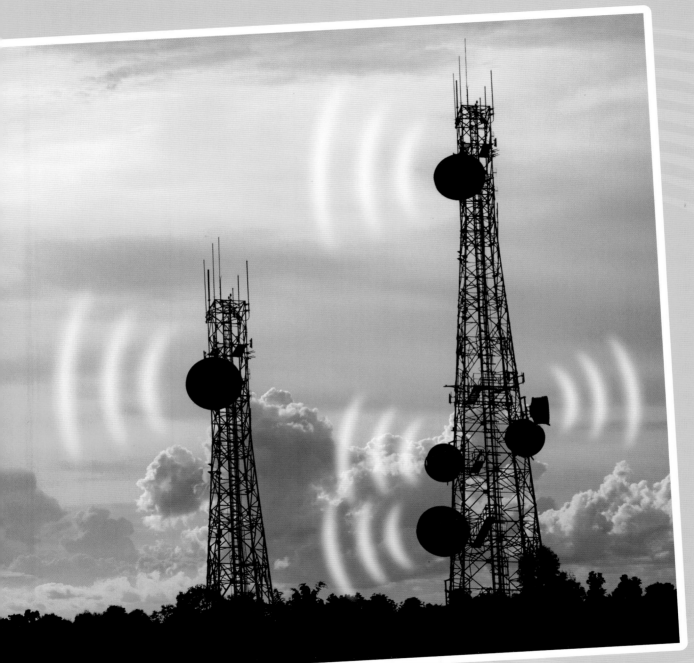

WAVES THAT SEE

Your mom tells you to take an umbrella to school. It's going to rain today. She saw it on the weather **radar** map on TV.

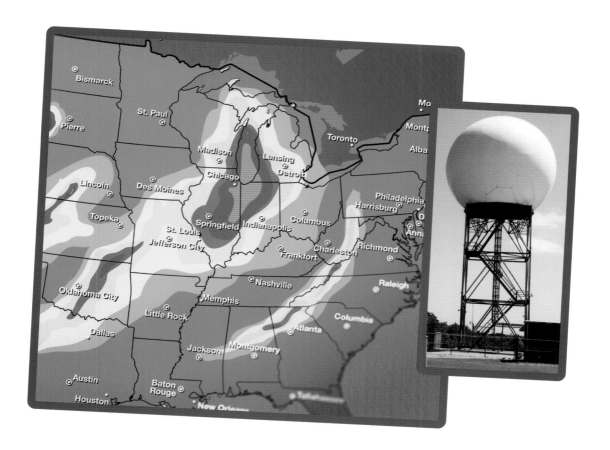

How does radar show that rain is coming? It starts with an **antenna**. The antenna turns in a circle. It sends microwaves through the air in all directions.

The microwaves travel until they hit rain or snow. Some of the waves go back to the antenna. These waves can tell us where the storm is. They can tell us how fast it's moving.

Microwaves help us cook food. They help us call friends. They even tell us about the weather. Microwaves help us every day in many ways!

TEST THE WAVES

The waves in a microwave oven bounce around. But they do not bounce evenly. Many microwave ovens come with a glass plate that spins inside. This is so microwaves can cover more of the food. Find out where the microwaves hit the food.

What You Need:

- a microwave oven with a glass plate
- four slices of bread
- butter or margarine spread

What You Do:

1. Take the glass plate out of the microwave oven. Turn it upside down.
2. Remove the ring that turns the plate.
3. Butter four slices of bread all over.
4. Put the bread side by side in two rows on the glass plate. The bread slices should touch.
5. Ask an adult to put the glass plate in the microwave oven.
6. Cook on full power for 20 seconds.
7. Have an adult take the glass plate out of the microwave oven.

How did the butter melt on the bread? Are there spots where the butter didn't melt? Why or why not?

GLOSSARY

antenna (an-TE-nuh)—a wire or dish that sends or receives signals

electricity (e-lek-TRI-si-tee)—form of energy used to make light and heat or to make machines work

energy (E-nuhr-jee)—the power to do work, such as moving things or giving heat or light

photon (FOH-tohn)—a unit of light

radar (RAY-dar)—a weather tool that sends out microwaves to find information about storms

signal (SIG-nuhl)—light, sound, or radio wave that sends information from place to place

vibrate (VYE-brate)—to quickly move back and forth

READ MORE

Diehn, Andi. *Waves: Physical Science for Kids.*
White River Junction, VT: Nomad Press, 2018.

Garstecki, Julia. *Light Waves.* North Mankato,
MN: Capstone, 2020.

Schuh, Mari. *Weather Patterns.* Vero Beach, FL:
Rourke Educational Media, 2019.

INTERNET SITES

Types of Electromagnetic Waves
https://www.ducksters.com/science/physics/
types_of_electromagnetic_waves.php

Facts About Microwaves
https://sciencewithkids.com/science-facts/facts-
about-microwaves.html

INDEX